THE JACOB'S LADDER

By the same author

POETRY

The Freeing of the Dust

Footprints

Life in the Forest

O Taste and See

Relearning the Alphabet

The Sorrow Dance

To Stay Alive

With Eyes at the Back of Our Heads

PROSE

The Poet in the World

TRANSLATIONS

Guillevic/ Selected Poems

The Ladder

Rabbi Moshe (of Kobryn) taught:
It is written: "And he dreamed,
and behold a ladder set up on the
earth." That "he" is every man.
Every man must know: I am clay,
I am one of countless shards of clay,
but "the top of it reached to
heaven"—my soul reaches to heaven; "and behold the angels of God
ascending and descending on it"—
even the ascent and descent of the
angels depend on my deeds.

Tales of the Hasidim: Later Masters by
Martin Buber.

The Jacob's Ladder

by

Denise Levertov

A New Directions Paperbook

Some of the poems in this book have appeared in the following magazines, to whom we give grateful thanks for permis-
sion to reprint: *Big Table, The Catholic Worker, Chelsea,
Chicago Choice, Damascus Road, Harper's, Hip Pocket
Poems, Jubilee, The Nation, Nomad, Origin, Outburst* (London), *Poetry, Quarterly Review, Quixote, Salon 13* (Guate-
mala), *San Francisco Review.*

The translation of two poems by Jules Supervielle are
published by courtesy of Librairie Gallimard, Paris.

The poems from *Overland to the Islands* are reprinted by
courtesy of the publisher, Jonathan Williams, Highlands,
North Carolina.

The quotation from *Tales of the Hasidim: Later Masters* by
Martin Buber, copyright 1948 by Shocken Books Inc., is
reprinted by courtesy of the publisher.

Manufactured in the United States of America

First published as New Directions Paperbook 112
(ISBN: 0-8112-0083-3), in December 1961.

New Directions Books are published for James Laughlin
by New Directions Publishing Corporation,
333 Sixth Avenue, New York 10014.

EIGHTH PRINTING

Contents

Poems from *Overland to the Islands* (1958)

To the Reader

As you read, a white bear leisurely
pees, dyeing the snow
saffron,

and as you read, many gods
lie among lianas: eyes of obsidian
are watching the generations of leaves,

and as you read
the sea is turning its dark pages,
turning
its dark pages.

A Common Ground

To stand on common ground
here and there gritty with pebbles
yet elsewhere 'fine and mellow—
uncommon fine for ploughing'

there to labor
planting the vegetable words
diversely in their order
that they come to virtue!

To reach those shining pebbles,
that soil where uncommon men
have labored in their virtue
and left a store

of seeds for planting!
To crunch on words
grown in grit or fine
crumbling earth, sweet

to eat and sweet
to be given, to be eaten
in common, by laborer
and hungry wanderer . . .

ii

In time of blossoming,
of red
buds, of red
margins upon
white petals among the
new green, of coppery
leaf-buds still weakly
folded, fuzzed
with silver hairs—

1

when on the grass verges
or elephant-hide rocks, the lunch hour
expands, the girls
laugh at the sun, men
in business suits awkwardly
recline, the petals
float and fall into
crumpled wax-paper, cartons
of hot coffee—

to speak as the sun's
deep tone of May gold speaks
or the spring chill in the rock's shadow,
a piercing minor scale running across the flesh
aslant—or petals
that dream their way
(speaking by being white
by being
curved, green-centered, falling
already while their tree
is half-red with buds) into

human lives! Poems stirred
into paper coffee-cups, eaten
with petals on rye in the
sun—the cold shadows in back,
and the traffic grinding the
borders of spring—entering
human lives forever,
unobserved, a spring element . . .

iii

. . . everything in the world must
excel itself to be itself.

Pasternak

Not 'common speech'
a dead level
but the uncommon speech of paradise,
tongue in which oracles
speak to beggars and pilgrims:

not illusion but what Whitman called
'the path
between reality and the soul,'
a language
excelling itself to be itself,

speech akin to the light
with which at day's end and day's
renewal, mountains
sing to each other across the cold valleys.

i

On the kitchen wall a flash
of shadow:
            swift pilgrimage
of pigeons, a spiral
celebration of air, of sky-deserts.
And on tenement windows
a blaze
            of lustered watermelon:
stain of the sun
westering somewhere back of Hoboken.

ii

The goatherd upstairs! Music
from his sweet flute
roves from summer to summer
in the dusty air of airshafts
and among the flakes
of soot that float
in a daze from chimney
to chimney—notes
remote, cool, speaking of slender
shadows under olive-leaves.   A silence.

iii

Groans, sighs, in profusion,
with coughing, muttering, orchestrate
solitary grief; the crash of glass, a low voice
repeating over and over, 'No.
No. I want my key. No you did not.
No.'—a commonplace.
And in counterpoint, from other windows,
the effort to be merry—ay, maracas!
—sibilant, intricate—the voices wailing pleasure,
        arriving perhaps at joy, late, after sets
have been switched off, and silences
are dark windows?

The Part

In some special way every person completes the universe. If he does not play his part, he injures the pattern of all existence. . . .

Rabbi Judah Loew

Homer da Vinci
with freckles on your nose
don't hang there

by the heels.
Sad everyman, I mean
let go, or jerk
upright.

They say gooseflesh
is the body's shudder when someone
walks over its grave-to-be,

but my hair rises
to see your living life
tamped down.

Blue mysteries
of the veronica florets
entertain
your modest attention:

there, where you live,
live:
start over,
everyman, with
the algae of your dreams.

Man gets his daily bread
in sweat, but no one said
in daily death. Don't eat

those nice green dollars your wife
gives you for breakfast.

i

A changing skyline.
A slice of window filled in
by a middle-distance oblong
topped by little
moving figures.
You are speaking
flatly, 'as one drinks a glass of

milk' (for calcium).
          Suddenly the milk
spills, a torrent of black milk hurtles
through the room, bubbling and
seething into the corners.

ii

'But then I was another person!'
The building veiled
in scaffolding. When the builders leave,
tenants will move in, pervading
cubic space with breath and dreams.
Odor of newmade memories
will loiter in the hallways,
noticed by helpless dogs and young children.
That will be other, another
building.

iii

I had meant to say
only, 'The skyline's changing,
the window's allowance of sky is
smaller
          but more
intensely designed, sprinkled
with human gestures.'

8

That's not enough.
Ah, if you've not seen it
it's not enough.
Alright.
It's true.
Nothing

is ever enough. Images
split the truth
in fractions. And milk
of speech is black lava. The sky
is sliced into worthless
glass diamonds.

iv

Again: middle of a night.
Silences lifting
bright eyes that brim with
smiles and painful
stone tears.
          Will you believe it,
in this very room
cloud-cuckoos unfledged themselves,
shedding feathers and down,
showed themselves small,
monstrous,
paltry in death?
In the dark
when the past lays its hand on your heart,
can't you recall that hour of
death and new daylight?

V

But how irrelevantly
the absurd angel of happiness walks in,
a box of matches in one hand,
in the other a book of dream-jokes.
I wake up laughing, tell you:
'I was writing an
ad for gold—gold cups,
gold porridge-bowls—**Gold,
beautiful, durable**—While I mused
for a third adjective, you were
preparing to leave for
three weeks—**Here's the check. And
perhaps in a week or so
I'll be able to send you a
pound of tomatoes.**' Then
you laugh too, and we clasp
in naked laughter, trembling
with tenderness and relief.
Meanwhile the angel,
dressed for laughs as a plasterer,
puts a match to whatever's
lying in the grate: broken scaffolds,
empty cocoons, the paraphernalia
of unseen change.
Our eyes smart from the smoke but
we laugh and
warm ourselves.

The Rainwalkers

An old man whose black face
shines golden-brown as wet pebbles
under the streetlamp, is walking
two mongrel dogs of dis-
proportionate size, in the rain,
in the relaxed early-evening avenue.

The small sleek one wants to stop,
docile to the imploring soul of the trashbasket,
but the young tall curly one
wants to walk on; the glistening sidewalk
entices him to arcane happenings.

Increasing rain. The old bareheaded man
smiles and grumbles to himself.
The lights change: the avenue's
endless nave echoes notes of
liturgical red. He drifts

between his dogs' desires.
The three of them are enveloped—
turning now to go crosstown—in their
sense of each other, of pleasure,
of weather, of corners,
of leisurely tensions between them
and private silence.

A doll's hair concealing
an eggshell skull delicately
throbbing, within which
maggots in voluptuous unrest
jostle and shrug. Oh, Eileen, my
big doll, your gold hair was
not more sunny than this
human fur, but
your head was
radiant in its emptiness,
a small clean room.

Her warm and rosy mouth
is telling lies—she would
believe them if she could believe:
her pretty eyes
search out corruption. Oh, Eileen,
how kindly your silence was, and
what virtue
shone in the opening and shutting of your
ingenious blindness.

The screendoor whines, clacks
shut.   My thoughts crackle
with seaweed-seething diminishing
flickers of phosphorus.   Gulp
of a frog, plash
of herring leaping;
                    interval;
squawk of a gull disturbed, a splashing;
pause
while silence poises for the breaking
bark of a seal: but silence.
                    Then
only your breathing. I'll
be quiet too. Out
stove, out lamp, let
night cut the question with profound
unanswer, sustained
echo of our unknowing.

While we sleep
mudflats will gleam
in moonwane, and mirror
     earliest wan daybreak
       in pockets and musselshell hillocks, before
a stuttering, through dreams, of
lobsterboats going out, a half-
awakening, a re-

living of ebbing dreams as morning ocean
returns to us, a turning
from light towards more dreams, intelligence of
what pulls at our depths for

design.
I hear

the tide turning. Last
eager wave over-
taken and pulled back
by first wave of the ebb. The pull back
by moon-ache. The great knots
of moon-awake energy
far out.

When the white fog burns off,
the abyss of everlasting light
is revealed. The last cobwebs
of fog in the
black firtrees are flakes
of white ash in the world's hearth.

Cold of the sea is counterpart
to this great fire. Plunging
out of the burning cold of ocean
we enter an ocean of intense
noon. Sacred salt
sparkles on our bodies.

After mist has wrapped us again
in fine wool, may the taste of salt
recall to us the great depths about us.

i

We have been shown
how Basket drank—
and old man Volpe the cobbler
made up what words he didn't know
so that his own son, even
laughed at him: but with respect.

ii

Two flutes! How close
to each other they move
in mazing figures,
never touching, never
breaking the measure,
as gnats dance in
summer haze all afternoon, over
shallow water sprinkled
with mottled blades of willow—
two flutes!

iii

Shlup, shlup, the dog
as it laps up
water
makes intelligent
music, resting
now and then to
take breath in irregular
measure.

iv

When I can't
strike one spark from you,
when you don't
look me in the eye,
when your answers
come
      slowly, dragging
their feet, and furrows
change your face,
when the sky is a cellar
with dirty windows,
when furniture
obstructs the body, and bodies
are heavy furniture coated
with dust—time
for a lagging leaden pace,
a short sullen line,
measure
of heavy heart and
cold eye.

v

The quick of the sun that gilds
broken pebbles in sidewalk cement
and the iridescent
spit; that defiles and adorns!
Gold light in blind love does not distinguish
one surface from another, the savor
is the same to its tongue, the fluted
cylinder of a new ashcan a dazzling silver,
the smooth flesh of screaming children a quietness, it is all
a jubilance, the light catches up
the disordered street in its apron,
broken fruitrinds shine in the gutter.

17

vi

Lap up the vowels
of sorrow,
        transparent, cold
water-darkness welling
up from the white sand.
Hone the blade
of a scythe to cut swathes
of light sound in the mind.
Through the hollow globe, a ring
of frayed rusty scrapiron,
is it the sea that shines?
Is it a road at the world's edge?

A Map of the Western Part of the
County of Essex in England

Something forgotten for twenty years: though my fathers
and mothers came from Cordova and Vitepsk and Caernarvon,
and though I am a citizen of the United States and less a
stranger here than anywhere else, perhaps,
I am Essex-born:
Cranbrook Wash called me into its dark tunnel,
the little streams of Valentines heard my resolves,
Roding held my head above water when I thought it was
drowning me; in Hainault only a haze of thin trees
stood between the red doubledecker buses and the boar-hunt,
the spirit of merciful Phillipa glimmered there.
Pergo Park knew me, and Clavering, and Havering-atte-
    Bower,
Stanford Rivers lost me in osier beds, Stapleford Abbots
sent me safe home on the dark road after Simeon-quiet
    evensong,
Wanstead drew me over and over into its basic poetry,
in its serpentine lake I saw bass-viols among the golden dead
    leaves,
through its trees the ghost of a great house. In
Ilford High Road I saw the multitudes passing pale under the
light of flaring sundown, seven kings
in somber starry robes gathered at Seven Kings
the place of law
where my birth and marriage are recorded
and the death of my father. Woodford Wells
where an old house was called The Naked Beauty (a white
statue forlorn in its garden)
saw the meeting and parting of two sisters,
(forgotten? and further away
the hill before Thaxted? where peace befell us? not once
but many times?).
All the Ivans dreaming of their villages
all the Marias dreaming of their walled cities,

picking up fragments of New World slowly,
not knowing how to put them together nor how to join
image with image, now I know how it was with you, an old map
    map
made long before I was born shows ancient
rights of way where I walked when I was ten burning with desire
    desire
for the world's great splendors, a child who traced voyages
indelibly all over the atlas, who now in a far country
remembers the first river, the first
field, bricks and lumber dumped in it ready for building,
that new smell, and remembers
the walls of the garden, the first light.

Come into Animal Presence

Come into animal presence.
No man is so guileless as
the serpent. The lonely white
rabbit on the roof is a star
twitching its ears at the rain.
The llama intricately
folding its hind legs to be seated
not disdains but mildly
disregards human approval.
What joy when the insouciant
armadillo glances at us and doesn't
quicken his trotting
across the track into the palm brush.

What is this joy? That no animal
falters, but knows what it must do?
That the snake has no blemish,
that the rabbit inspects his strange surroundings
in white star-silence? The llama
rests in dignity, the armadillo
has some intention to pursue in the palm-forest.
Those who were sacred have remained so,
holiness does not dissolve, it is a presence
of bronze, only the sight that saw it
faltered and turned from it.
An old joy returns in holy presence.

In the autumn brilliance
feathers tingle at fingertips.

This tingling brilliance
burns under cover of gray air and

brown lazily
unfalling leaves,

it eats into stillness zestfully
with sound of plucked strings,

steel and brass strings of the zither,
copper and silver wire

played with a gold ring,
a plucking of crinkled afternoons and

evenings of energy, thorns under the pot.
In the autumn brilliance

a drawing apart of curtains
a fall of veils

a flying open of doors, convergence
of magic objects into
feathered hands and crested heads, a prospect
of winter verve, a buildup to abundance.

Song for a Dark Voice

My black sun, my
Odessa sunflower,
spurs of Tartar gold
ring at your ankles,
you stand taller before me than the ten
towers of Jerusalem.

Your tongue has found
my tongue, peonies
turn their profusion towards
the lamp, it is you that burn there,
the Black Sea sings you awake.

Wake the violoncellos of Lebanon,
rub the bows with cedar resin,
wake the Tundra horsemen
to hunt tigers.
          Your skin
tastes of the salt of Marmora,
the hair of your body casts
its net over me.
          To my closed eyes
appears a curved
horizon where darkness
dazzles in your light. Your arms
hold me from falling.

A Window

Among a hundred windows shining
    dully in the vast side
of greater-than-palace number such-and-such
    one burns
these several years, each night
    as if the room within were aflame.
Some fault in the glass
    combines with the precise distance and
my faulty eyes to produce
    this illusion; I know it—
yet still I'm ready to believe perhaps
    some lives
tremble and flare up there, four blocks away
    across the sooty roofs and
the dusk,
    with more intensity than what's lived
behind the other windows,
    and the glowing of those brands of life
shows as seraphic or demonic flames
    visible only to weak and distant eyes.

'. . .Else a great Prince in prison lies'

All that blesses the step of the antelope
all the grace a giraffe lifts to the highest leaves
all steadfastness and pleasant gazing, alien to ennui,
dwell secretly behind man's misery.

Animal face, when the lines
of human fear, knots of a net, become transparent
and your brilliant eyes and velvet muzzle
are revealed, who shall say you are not the face of a man?

In the dense light of wakened flesh
animal man is a prince. As from alabaster
a lucency animates him from heel to forehead.
Then his shadows are deep and not gray.

i   The Weave

The cowdung-colored mud
baked and raised up in random
walls, bears the silken
lips and lashes of erotic
flowers towards a sky of
noble clouds. Accepted
sacramental excrement
supports the ecstatic half-sleep
of butterflies, the slow
opening and closing of brilliant
dusty wings. Bite down
on the bitter stem of your nectared
rose, you know
the dreamy stench of death and fling
magenta shawls delicately
about your brown shoulders laughing.

ii   Corazón

When in bushy hollows between
moonround and moonround of hill, white clouds
loiter arm-in-arm, out of curl,
and sheep in the ravines
vaguely congregate, the heart
of Mexico sits in the rain
not caring to seek shelter,
a blanket of geranium pink drawn up
over his silent mouth.

iii   The Rose
(*for B.L.*)

In the green Alameda, near the fountains,
an old man, hands
clasped behind his shabby back
shuffles from rose to rose, stopping
to ponder and inhale, and I
follow him at a distance, discovering
the golden rose, color of bees' fur, odor of honey,
red rose, contralto, roses
of dawn-cloud-color, of snow-in-moonlight,
of colors only roses know,
but no rose
like the rose I saw in your garden.

iv   Canticle

Flies, acolytes
of the death-in-life temple
buzz their prayers

and from the altar
of excrement arises
an incense

of orange and purple
petals.   Drink,
campesino,

stain with ferment
the blinding white that clothes
your dark body.

v Sierra

Golden the high ridge of thy back, bull-mountain,
and coffee-black thy full sides.
The sky decks thy horns with violet,
with cascades of cloud. The brown hills
are thy cows.   Shadows
of zopilotes cross and slowly
cross again
thy flanks, lord of herds.

Three Meditations

i

the only object is
a man, carved
out of himself, so wrought he
fills his given space, makes
traceries sufficient to
others' needs
            (here is
social action, for the poet,
anyway, his
politics, his
news)

Charles Olson

Breathe deep of the
freshly gray morning air, mild
spring of the day.
Let the night's dream-planting
bear leaves
and light up the death-mirrors with
shining petals.
Stand fast in thy place:
remember, Caedmon
turning from song was met
in his cow-barn by One who set him
to sing the beginning.
Live
in thy fingertips and in thy
hair's rising; hunger
be thine, food
be thine and what wine
will not shrivel thee.
Breathe deep of
evening, be with the
rivers of tumult, sharpen
thy wits to know power and be
humble.

29

ii

The task of the poet is to make clear
to *himself,* and thereby to others,
the temporal and eternal questions.

Ibsen

Barbarians
throng the straight roads of
my empire, converging
on black Rome.
There is darkness in me.
Silver sunrays
sternly, in tenuous joy
cut through its folds:
mountains
arise from cloud.
Who was it yelled, cracking
the glass of delight?
Who sent the child
sobbing to bed, and woke it
later to comfort it?
I, I, I, I.
I multitude, I tyrant,
I angel, I you, you
world, battlefield, stirring
with unheard litanies, sounds of piercing
green half-smothered by
strewn bones.

iii

And virtue? Virtue lies in the heroic
response to the creative wonder, the
utmost response.

D. H. Lawrence

Death in the grassblade
a dull
substance, heading blindly
for the bone

30

and bread preserved without
virtue,
sweet grapes sour to the children's children.

We breathe an ill wind,
nevertheless our kind
in mushroom multitudes
jostles for elbow-room
moonwards

an equalization of
hazards
bringing the poet
back to song
as before

to sing of death
as before
and life, while he
has it, energy

being in him a singing,
a beating of gongs, efficacious
to drive away devils,
response to

the wonder that
as before
shows a double face,

to be
what he is
being his virtue

filling his whole space
so no devil
may enter.

i

The day before he died, a burnet moth
come to town perhaps on a load of greens,
took me a half-hour out of my way, or what
I'd thought was my way.   It lay bemused
on the third step down of the subway entrance.
I took it up—it scarcely fluttered. Where
should I take it for safety,
away from hasty feet and rough hands?
We went through the hot streets together,
it lay trustingly in my hand,
awkwardly I shielded it from the dusty
wind, a glitter of brine
hovered about the cement vistas.
At last I found
a scrap of green garden
to hide the stranger, and silently took leave.

Not his soul—
I knew that dwelled always on Russian earth
—yet it was spoken in me
that the dark, narrow-winged, richly
crimson-signed being, an
apparition at the steps to the underworld,
whose need took me upwards again and further than
I had thought to walk, was a word,
an emanation from him, fulfilling
what he had written—'I feel
that we shall be friends.'

ii

Seen through what seem
his eyes (his gift) the gray barn
and the road into the forest,
the snipe's dead young I am burying among
wild-strawberry leaves, all
lifts itself, poises itself to speak:

and the deaf soul
struggles, strains forward, to lip-read what it needs:
and something is said, quickly,
in words of cloud-shadows moving and
the unmoving turn of the road, something
not quite caught, but filtered
through some outpost of dreaming sense
the gist, the drift. I remember
a dream two nights ago: the voice,
'the artist must
create himself or be born again.'

(after Jules Supervielle)

That sound, everywhere about us, of the sea—
the tree among its tresses has always heard it,
and the horse dips his black body in the sound
stretching his neck as if towards drinking water,
as if he were longing to leave the dunes and become
a mythic horse in the remotest distance,
joining the flock of foam-sheep—
fleeces made for vision alone—
to be indeed the son of these salt waters
and browse on algae in the deep fields.
But he must learn to wait, wait on the shore,
promising himself **someday** to the waves of the open sea,
putting his hope in certain death, lowering
his head again to the grass.

(after Jules Supervielle)

A poplar tree under the stars,
what can it do.
And the bird in the poplar tree
dreaming, his head
tucked into
far-and-near exile under his wing—
what can either of them
in their confused alliance of
leaves and feathers
do to avert destiny?

Silence and the
ring of forgetting
protect them until the moment when
the sun rises
and memory with it.
Then the bird
breaks with his beak the thread
of dream within him,
and the tree unrolls
the shadow that will guard it
throughout the day.

The head Byzantine or from
Fayyum, the shoulders naked,
a little of the
dark-haired breast visible
above the sheet,

from deep in the dark head
his smile glowing
outward into the
room's severe twilight,

he lies, a dark-shadowed
mellow gold against
the flattened white pillow,
a gentle man—

strength and despair
quiet there in the bed,
the line of his limbs
half-shown, as under stone
or bronze folds.

The Jacob's Ladder

The stairway is not
a thing of gleaming strands
a radiant evanescence
for angels' feet that only glance in their tread, and need not
touch the stone.

It is of stone.
A rosy stone that takes
a glowing tone of softness
only because behind it the sky is a doubtful, a doubting
night gray.

A stairway of sharp
angles, solidly built.
One sees that the angels must spring
down from one step to the next, giving a little
lift of the wings:

and a man climbing
must scrape his knees, and bring
the grip of his hands into play. The cut stone
consoles his groping feet. Wings brush past him.
The poem ascends.

The Muse
   in her dark habit,
trim-waisted,
   wades into deep water.

The spring where she
   will fill her pitcher to the brim
wells out
   below the lake's surface, among
papyrus, where a stream
   enters the lake and is crossed
by the bridge on which I stand.

She stoops
   to gently dip and deep enough.
Her face resembles
   the face of the young actress who played
Miss Annie Sullivan, she who
   spelled the word 'water' into the palm
of Helen Keller, opening
   the doors of the world.

In the baroque park,
   transformed as I neared the water
   to Valentines, a place of origin,
I stand on a bridge of one span
and see this calm act, this gathering up
   of life, of spring water

and the Muse gliding then
   in her barge without sails, without
oars or motor, across
   the dark lake, and I know

no interpretation of these mysteries
   although I know she is the Muse
and that the humble
   tributary of Roding is
one with Alpheus, the god who as a river
   flowed through the salt sea to his love's well

so that my heart leaps
   in wonder.
Cold, fresh, deep, I feel the word 'water'
   spelled in my left palm.

Months after the Muse
had come and gone across the lake of vision,
arose out of childhood the long-familiar
briefly forgotten presaging of her image—

'The Light of Truth'—frontispiece
to 'Parables from Nature,' 1894—a picture
intending another meaning than that which it gave
(for I never read the story until now)

intending to represent Folly
sinking into a black bog, but for me having meant
a mystery, of darkness, of beauty, of serious
dreaming pause and intensity

where not a will-o'-the-wisp but
a star come to earth burned before the
closed all-seeing eyes
of that figure later seen as the Muse.

By which I learn to affirm
Truth's light at strange turns of the mind's road,
wrong turns that lead
over the border into wonder,

mistaken directions, forgotten signs
all bringing the soul's travels to a place
of origin, a well
under the lake where the Muse moves.

i

Osip Mandelstam

With a glass of
boiled water
not yet cold
by a small stove
not giving out
much heat
he was sitting
and saying over
those green words
Laura and laurel
written in Avignon

when out of the somber
winter day entered
Death in green clothing
having traveled
by train and on foot
ten thousand kilometers to
this end,
and moving aside to give him
a place at the fire, the poet
made him welcome, asking
for news of home.

ii
César Vallejo

Darling Death
shouted in his ear,
his ear made to record
the least, the most finespun
of worm-cries and
dragonfly-jubilations,
and with that courtesy he accorded
all clumsy living things
that stumble in broken boots
he bowed and
not flinching from her black breath
gave her his arm and
walked back with her the
way she had come and
turned the corner.

Melody
> moving
> > downstream
a string of barges
> > just
lit
against blue evening, the fog
giving each light
a halo

moving with
the river but not
adrift, a little
> faster perhaps
> or is it
slower? —a
singing
sung if it is sung
quietly

within the scored
crashing and the
almost inaudible hum impinging
upon the river's
> > seawardness

A Letter to William Kinter of Muhlenberg

Zaddik, you showed me
the Stations of the Cross

and I saw
not what the almost abstract

tiles held—world upon world—
but at least

a shadow of what
might be seen there if mind and heart

gave themselves to meditation,
deeper

and deeper into Imagination's
holy forest, as travelers

followed the Zohar's dusty
shimmering roads, talking

with prophets and
hidden angels.

From the bus, Zaddik,
going home to New York,

I saw a new world
for a while—it was

the gold light on a rocky slope,
the road-constructors talking to each other,

44

bear-brown of winter woods, and later
lights of New Jersey factories and the vast

December moon. I saw
without words within me, saw

as if my eyes
had grown bigger and knew

how to look without
being told what it was they saw.

The clouds as I see them, rising
urgently, roseate in the
mounting of somber power

surging in evening haste over
roofs and hermetic
grim walls—

       Last night
as if death had lit a pale light
in your flesh, your flesh
was cold to my touch, or not cold
but cool, cooling, as if the last traces
of warmth were still fading in you.
My thigh burned in cold fear where
yours touched it.

But I forced to mind my vision of a sky
close and enclosed, unlike the space in which these clouds
     move—
a sky of gray mist it appeared—
and how looking intently at it we saw
its gray was not gray but a milky white
in which radiant traces of opal greens,
fiery blues, gleamed, faded, gleamed again,
and how only then, seeing the color in the gray,
a field sprang into sight, extending
between where we stood and the horizon,

a field of freshest deep spiring grass
starred with dandelions,
green and gold
gold and green alternating in closewoven
chords, madrigal field.

Is death's chill that visited our bed
other than what it seemed, is it
a gray to be watched keenly?

Wiping my glasses and leaning westward,
clearing my mind of the day's mist and leaning
into myself to see
the colors of truth

I watch the clouds as I see them
in pomp advancing, pursuing
the fallen sun.

The Thread

Something is very gently,
invisibly, silently,
pulling at me—a thread
or net of threads
finer than cobweb and as
elastic. I haven't tried
the strength of it. No barbed hook
pierced and tore me. Was it
not long ago this thread
began to draw me? Or
way back? Was I
born with its knot about my
neck, a bridle? Not fear
but a stirring
of wonder makes me
catch my breath when I feel
the tug of it when I thought
it had loosened itself and gone.

From the Roof

This wild night, gathering the washing as if it were flowers
            animal vines twisting over the line and
            slapping my face lightly, soundless merriment
            in the gesticulations of shirtsleeves,
I recall out of my joy a night of misery

walking in the dark and the wind over broken earth,
            halfmade foundations and unfinished
            drainage trenches and the spaced-out
                      circles of glaring light
            marking streets that were to be,
walking with you but so far from you,

and now alone in October's
first decision towards winter, so close to you—
            my arms full of playful rebellious linen, a freighter
            going down-river two blocks away, outward bound,
            the green wolf-eyes of the Harborside Terminal
                   glittering on the Jersey shore,
and a train somewhere under ground bringing you towards me
to our new living-place from which we can see

a river and its traffic (the Hudson and the
hidden river, who can say which it is we see, we see
something of both. Or who can say
the crippled broom-vendor yesterday, who passed
just as we needed a new broom, was not
one of the Hidden Ones?)

Crates of fruit are unloading
across the street on the cobbles,
and a brazier flaring
    to warm the men and burn trash. He wished us
luck when we bought the broom. But not luck
brought us here. By design

clear air and cold wind polish
the river lights, by design
we are to live now in a new place.

The Presence

To the house on the grassy hill
where rams rub their horns against the porch

and your bare feet on the floors of silence
speak in rhymed stanzas to the furniture,

solemn chests of drawers and heavy chairs
blinking in the sun you have let in!

Before I enter the rooms of your solitude
in my living form, trailing my shadow,

I shall have come unseen. Upstairs and down with you
and out across road and rocks to the river

to drink the cold spray. You will believe
a bird flew by the window, a wandering bee

buzzed in the hallway, a wind
rippled the bronze grasses. Or will you

know who it is?

To go by the asters
and breathe
the sweetness that hovers

in August about the tall milkweeds,
without a direct look, seeing
only obliquely what we know

is there—that
sets the heart beating fast!
And through

the field of goldenrod,
the lazily-humming waves of
standing hay, not to look up

at the sea-green bloom on the mountain—
the lips part, a sense
of languor and strength begins

to mount in us. The path leads
to the river pool, cold and
flashing with young trout. The sun

on my whiteness and your
tawny gold. Without looking
I see through my lashes the iridescence

on black curls of sexual hair.

The Tulips

Red tulips
living into their death
flushed with a wild blue

tulips
becoming wings
ears of the wind
jackrabbits rolling their eyes

west wind
shaking the loose pane

some petals fall
with that sound one
listens for

In Sabbath quiet, a street
of closed warehouses and wholesale silence,
Adam Misery, while the cop frisks him

lifts with both hands his lip and
drooping mustache to reveal
horse-teeth for inspection.

                    Nothing
is new to him and he is not afraid.
This is a world. As the artist

extends his world with
one gratuitous flourish—a stroke of white or
a run on the clarinet above the

bass tones of the orchestra—so he
ornaments his with
fresh contempt.

The Fountain

Don't say, don't say there is no water
to solace the dryness at our hearts.
I have seen

the fountain springing out of the rock wall
and you drinking there. And I too
before your eyes

found footholds and climbed
to drink the cool water.

The woman of that place, shading her eyes,
frowned as she watched—but not because
she grudged the water,

only because she was waiting
to see we drank our fill and were
refreshed.

Don't say, don't say there is no water.
That fountain is there among its scalloped
green and gray stones,

it is still there and always there
with its quiet song and strange power
to spring in us,
up and out through the rock.

From love one takes
petal to **rock** and **blesséd**
away towards
descend,

one took thought
for frail tint and spectral
glisten, trusted
from way back that stillness,

one knew
that heart of fire, rose
at the core of gold glow,
could go down undiminished,

for love and
or if in fear knowing
the risk, knowing
what one is touching, one does it,

each part
of speech a spark
awaiting redemption, each
a virtue, a power

in abeyance unless we
give it care
our need designs in us. Then
all we have led away returns to us.

i

The authentic! Shadows of it
sweep past in dreams, one could say imprecisely,
evoking the almost-silent
ripping apart of giant
sheets of cellophane. No.
It thrusts up close. Exactly in dreams
it has you off-guard, you
recognize it before you have time.
For a second before waking
the alarm bell is a red conical hat, it
takes form.

ii

The authentic! I said
rising from the toilet seat.
The radiator in rhythmic knockings
spoke of the rising steam.
The authentic, I said
breaking the handle of my hairbrush as I
brushed my hair in
rhythmic strokes: That's it,
that's joy, it's always
a recognition, the known
appearing fully itself, and
more itself than one knew.

iii

The new day rises
as heat rises,

knocking in the pipes
with rhythms it seizes for its own
to speak of its invention—
the real, the new-laid
egg whose speckled shell
the poet fondles and must break
if he will be nourished.

iv

A shadow painted where
yes, a shadow must fall.
The cow's breath
not forgotten in the mist, in the
words. Yes,
verisimilitude draws up
heat in us, zest
to follow through,
follow through,
follow
transformations of day
in its turning, in its becoming.

v

Stir the holy grains, set
the bowls on the table and
call the child to eat.

While we eat we think,
as we think an undercurrent
of dream runs through us
faster than thought
towards recognition.

Call the child to eat,
send him off, his mouth
tasting of toothpaste, to go down
into the ground, into a roaring train
and to school.

His cheeks are pink
his black eyes hold his dreams, he has left
forgetting his glasses.

Follow down the stairs at a clatter
to give them to him and save
his clear sight.

Cold air
comes in at the street door.

vi

The authentic! It rolls
just out of reach, beyond
running feet and
stretching fingers, down
the green slope and into
the black waves of the sea.
Speak to me, little horse, beloved,
tell me
how to follow the iron ball,
how to follow through to the country
beneath the waves
to the place where I must kill you and you step out
of your bones and flystrewn meat
tall, smiling, renewed,
formed in your own likeness

vii

Marvelous Truth, confront us
at every turn,
in every guise, iron ball,
egg, dark horse, shadow,
cloud
of breath on the air,

dwell
in our crowded hearts
our steaming bathrooms, kitchens full of
things to be done, the
ordinary streets.

Thrust close your smile
that we know you, terrible joy.

During the Eichmann Trial

i When We Look Up

> When we look up
> each from his being
> *Robert Duncan*

He had not looked,
pitiful man whom none

pity, whom all
must pity if they look

into their own face (given
only by glass, steel, water

barely known) all
who look up

to see—how many
faces?   How many

seen in a lifetime? (Not those
that flash by, but those

into which the gaze wanders
and is lost

and returns to tell
Here is a mystery,

**a person, an
other, an I?**

Count them.
Who are five million?)

'I was used from the nursery
to obedience

all my life . . .
Corpselike

obedience.' Yellow
calmed him later—

'a charming picture'
yellow of autumn leaves in

Wienerwald, a little
railroad station
nineteen-o-eight, Lemburg,

yellow sun
on the stepmother's teatable

Franz Joseph's beard
blessing his little ones.

It was the yellow
of the stars too,

stars that marked
those in whose faces

you had not
looked. 'They were cast out

as if they were
some animals, some beasts.'

'And what would disobedience
have brought me? And

whom would it have served?'
'I did not let my thoughts

dwell on this—I had
seen it and that was

enough.' (The words
'slur into a harsh babble')

'A spring of blood
gushed from the earth.'
Miracle

unsung. I see
a spring of blood gush from the earth—

Earth cannot swallow
so much at once

a fountain
rushes towards the sky

unrecognized
a sign—.

Pity this man who saw it
whose obedience continued—

he, you, I, which shall I say?
He stands

isolate in a bulletproof
witness-stand of glass,

a cage, where we may view
ourselves, an apparition

telling us something he
does not know: we are members

one of another.

ii   The Peachtree

The Danube orchards
are full of fruit
but in the city one tree
haunts a boy's dreams

a tree in a villa garden
the Devil's garden
a peach tree

and of its fruit one peach
calls to him

he sees it yellow and ripe
the vivid blood
bright in its round cheek

Next day he knows
he cannot withstand desire
it is no common fruit

it holds some secret
it speaks to the yellow star within him

he scales the wall
enters the garden of death
takes the peach
and death pounces

mister death who rushes out
from his villa
mister death who loves yellow

who wanted that yellow peach
for himself
mister death who signs papers
then eats

telegraphs simply: **Shoot them**
then eats
mister death who orders
more transports
then eats

he would have enjoyed
the sweetest of all the peaches on his tree
with sour-cream
with brandy

Son of David
's blood, vivid red
and trampled juice
yellow and sweet
flow together beneath the tree

there is more blood than
sweet juice
always more blood—mister
death goes indoors
exhausted

Note: This poem is based on the earliest mention, during the trial, of
this incident. In a later statement it was said that the fruit was cherries,
that the boy was already in the garden, doing forced labor, when he
was accused of taking the fruit, and that Eichmann killed him in a tool
shed, not beneath the tree. The poem therefore is not to be taken as a
report of what happened but of what I envisioned.

iii   Crystal Night

From blacked-out streets
    (wide avenues swept by curfew,
    alleyways, veins
    of dark within dark)

from houses whose walls
    had for a long time known
the tense stretch of skin over bone
as their brick or stone listened—

            The scream!
The awaited scream rises,
the shattering
of glass and the cracking
of bone

a polar tumult as when
black ice booms, knives
of ice and glass
splitting and splintering the silence into
innumerable screaming needles of
yes, now it is upon us, the jackboots
are running in spurts of
sudden blood-light through the
broken temples

the veils
are rent in twain

terror has a white sound
every scream
of fear is a white needle freezing the eyes
the floodlights of their trucks throw
jets of white, their shouts
cleave the wholeness of darkness into
sectors of transparent white-clouded pantomime
where all that was awaited
is happening, it is Crystal Night

it is Crystal Night
these spikes which are not
pitched in the range of common hearing
whistle through time

smashing the windows of sleep and dream
smashing the windows of history
a whiteness scattering
in hailstones
each a mirror
for man's eyes.

A blind man. I can stare at him
ashamed, shameless. Or does he know it?
No, he is in a great solitude.

O, strange joy,
to gaze my fill at a stranger's face.
No, my thirst is greater than before.

In his world he is speaking
almost aloud. His lips move.
Anxiety plays about them. And now joy

of some sort trembles into a smile.
A breeze I can't feel
crosses that face as if it crossed water.

The train moves uptown, pulls in and
pulls out of the local stops. Within its loud
jarring movement a quiet,

the quiet of people not speaking,
some of them eyeing the blind man,
only a moment though, not thirsty like me,

and within that quiet his
different quiet, not quiet at all, a tumult
of images, but what are his images,

he is blind? He doesn't care
that he looks strange, showing
his thoughts on his face like designs of light

flickering on water, for he doesn't know
what **look** is.
I see he has never seen.

And now he rises, he stands at the door ready,
knowing his station is next. Was he counting?
No, that was not his need.

When he gets out I get out.
'Can I help you towards the exit?'
'Oh, alright.' An indifference.

But instantly, even as he speaks,
even as I hear indifference, his hand
goes out, waiting for me to take it,

and now we hold hands like children.
His hand is warm and not sweaty,
the grip firm, it feels good.

And when we have passed through the turnstile,
he going first, his hand at once
waits for mine again.

'Here are the steps. And here we turn
to the right. More stairs now.' We go
up into sunlight. He feels that,

the soft air. 'A nice day,
isn't it?' says the blind man. Solitude
walks with me, walks

beside me, he is not with me, he continues
his thoughts alone. But his hand and mine
know one another,

it's as if my hand were gone forth
on its own journey. I see him
across the street, the blind man,

and now he says he can find his way. He knows
where he is going, it is nowhere, it is filled
with presences. He says, **I am.**

Poems from *Overland to the Islands*

(1958)

Overland to the Islands

Let's go—much as that dog goes,
intently haphazard. The
Mexican light on a day that
'smells like autumn in Connecticut'
makes iris ripples on his
black gleaming fur—and that too
is as one would desire—a radiance
consorting with the dance.
                    Under his feet
rocks and mud, his imagination, sniffing,
engaged in its perceptions—dancing
edgeways, there's nothing
the dog disdains on his way,
nevertheless he
keeps moving, changing
pace and approach but
not direction—'every step an arrival.'

Scenes from the Life of the Peppertrees

i

The peppertrees, the peppertrees!

Cats are stretching in the doorways,
sure of everything. It is morning.
    But the peppertrees
stand aside in diffidence, with berries
of modest red.
                Branch above branch, an air
of lightness; of shadows
scattered lightly.
           A cat
closes upon its shadow.
Up and up goes the sun,
sure of everything.
    The peppertrees
           shiver a little.
Robust
and soot-black, the cat
leaps to a low branch. Leaves
close about him.

ii

The yellow moon dreamily
tipping buttons of light
down among the leaves. Marimba,
marimba—from beyond the
black street.
           Somebody dancing,
somebody
        getting the hell
outta here. Shadows of cats
weave round the tree trunks,
the exposed knotty roots.

74

iii

The man on the bed sleeping
defenseless. Look—
his bare long feet together
sideways, keeping each other
warm. And the foreshortened shoulders,
the head
barely visible.   He is good.
let him sleep.
               But the third peppertree
    is restless, twitching
thin leaves in the light
of afternoon.   After a while
it walks over and taps
on the upstairs window with a bunch
of red berries.   Will he wake?

The Whirlwind

The doors keep rattling—I
stick poems between their teeth to
stop them. The brown dust
twirls up outside the window, off
the dead jicama field, scares the curtains,
spirals away to the dirty hollow
where the cesspools are, and the most ants,
and beyond—to the unfenced pasture land, where nothing
will get in its way for miles and it
can curtsey itself at last into
some arroyo.   The doors
keep rattling—I'm
shivering, desperate for a poem
to stuff into their maws that will
silence them. I know what they want:
they want
in all their wooden strength
to fly off on the whirlwind into
the great nothingness.

One A.M.

The kitchen patio in snowy
moonlight.   That
snowsilence, that
abandon to stillness.
The sawhorse, the concrete
washtub, snowblue. The washline
bowed under its snowfur!
Moon has silenced
the crickets, the summer frogs
hold their breath.
Summer night, summer night, standing
one-legged, a crane
in the snowmarsh, staring
at snowmoon!

Here I lie asleep
or maybe I'm awake yet—

not alone—and yet
it seems by moonlight

I'm alone, hardly hearing
a breath beside me. And those shadows

on the wall indeed are
not shadows but the
featherweight dancing echoes
of headlights sliding by.

Here I lie and wonder
what it is has left me, what element.
I can't remember my dreams
by morning.
        Maybe, as Frazer tells,

my soul flew out in that moment
of almost-sleep.   If it should go
back to the scenes and times
of its wars and losses

how would I ever lure it
back? It would

be looking for something, it would be
too concentrated to hear me.

O moon, watching everything,
delay it in the garden among the white flowers

until the cold air before sunrise
makes it glad to come back to me through the screens.

Lonely Man

An open world
　　　within its mountain rim:
trees on the plain lifting
　　　their heads, fine strokes
　　　of grass stretching themselves to breathe
the last of the light.
　　　　　　Where a man
riding horseback raises dust
　　　under the eucalyptus trees, a long way off, the dust
is gray-gold, a cloud
　　　of pollen. A field
　　　of cosmea turns
　　　all its many faces
of wide-open flowers west, to the light.

It is your loneliness
your energy
　　　　baffled in the stillness
　　　gives an edge to the shadows—
the great sweep of mountain shadow,
shadows of ants and leaves,
　　　the stones of the road each with its shadow
and you with your long shadow
closing your book and standing up
to stretch, your long shadow-arms
　　　stretching back of you, baffled.

As if it were
forever that they move, that we
keep moving—

Under a wan sky where
as the lights went on a star
pierced the haze & now
follows steadily
a constant
above our six lanes
the dreamlike continuum . . .

And the people—ourselves!
the humans from inside the
cars, apparent
only at gasoline stops
unsure,
eyeing each other

drink coffee hastily at the
slot machines & hurry
back to the cars
vanish
into them forever, to
keep moving—

Houses now & then beyond the
sealed road, the trees / trees, bushes
passing by, passing
   the cars that
     keep moving ahead of
  us, past us, pressing behind us
           and
     over left, those that come
   toward us shining too brightly
moving relentlessly

  in six lanes, gliding
 north & south, speeding with
 a slurred sound—

The shifting, the shaded
    change of pleasure

Soft warm ashes in place of fire
    out, irremediably

and a door blown open:

planes tilt, interact, objects
    fuse, disperse,
    this chair further from that table . . . hold it!
    Focus on that: this table
    closer to that shadow. It's what appalls the
    heart's red rust. Turn, turn!
    Loyalty betrays.

        It's the fall of it, the drift,
           pleasure
        source and sequence
           lift
        of golden cold sea.

The Springtime

The red eyes of rabbits
aren't sad. No one passes
the sad golden village in a barge
any more. The sunset
will leave it alone. If the
curtains hang askew
it is no one's fault.
Around and around and around
everywhere the same sound
of wheels going, and things
growing older, growing
silent. If the dogs
bark to each other
all night, and their eyes
flash red, that's
nobody's business. They have
a great space of dark to
bark across. The rabbits
will bare their teeth at
the spring moon.

A stir in the air, the proper space
holding existences in grave distinction—
If as you read I walk
          around you in a
                half circle
your response to the poem will
waver, maybe, like the lights just now
in the thunderstorm—the balance
is that fine—the dance
of hiving bees it is, that design
in air, joyfully
          reducing possibilities to
                          one, the next act.

Sunday Afternoon

After the First Communion
and the banquet of mangoes and
bridal cake, the young daughters
of the coffee merchant lay down
for a long siesta, and their white dresses
lay beside them in quietness
and the white veils floated
in their dreams as the flies buzzed.
But as the afternoon
burned to a close they rose
and ran about the neighborhood
among the halfbuilt villas
alive, alive, kicking a basketball, wearing
other new dresses, of bloodred velvet.

Since the storm two nights ago
the air
is water-clear, the mountains
tranquil and clear.
    Have you seen
an intelligent invalid—that look
about the eyes and temples?—one who
knows damn well
death is coming—in the guise let's say
of a carpenter, coming
to fix him for good
with his big hammer and
sharp nails.
    The air and the horizon.
Clouds make
  gestures of flight but
remain suspended. The builders
continue to build the
house next door.
    Nothing
will happen. A transparence
of the flesh, revealing
not bones but the shape of bones.

The Rav
of Northern White Russia declined,
in his youth, to learn the
language of birds, because
the extraneous did not interest him; nevertheless
when he grew old it was found
he understood them anyway, having
listened well, and as it is said, 'prayed
                    with the bench and the floor.' He used
what was at hand—as did
Angel Jones of Mold, whose meditations
were sewn into coats and britches.
                    Well, I would like to make,
thinking some line still taut between me and them,
poems direct as what the birds said,
hard as a floor, sound as a bench,
mysterious as the silence when the tailor
would pause with his needle in the air.

DENISE LEVERTOV, whose mother is Welsh and whose father, an Anglican clergyman, was by birth a Russian Jew, was born in 1923 in London and grew up in suburban Ilford, Essex. She was educated at home (never attending school or college), studied ballet for a time, and worked as a nurse during the war. Married to the writer Mitchell Goodman in 1947, she came to the United States the following year. Their son Nikolai was born in 1949.

Miss Levertov has read her poems at many colleges, as well as the Poetry Centers of New York and San Francisco. During 1961 and again from 1963 through 1965 she served as Poetry Editor of *The Nation*. She has taught at Drew University, C.C.N.Y., the Poetry Center (YMHA, New York), Vassar College and the University of California at Berkeley. She has been a Guggenheim Fellow, a Scholar of the Radcliffe Institute for Independent Study, and the recipient of a National Institute of Arts and Letters grant.

The poet's first book, *The Double Image*, was published by the Cresset Press, London, in 1946. Her first American publication was in *The New British Poets*, an anthology edited by Kenneth Rexroth, published in 1948 by New Directions. Since then, she has been considered an American poet and has published *Here and Now* (City Lights, 1957), *Overland to The Islands* (Jargon Books, 1958), *With Eyes At The Back of Our Heads* (New Directions, 1960), *The Jacob's Ladder* (New Directions, 1961), *O Taste and See* (New Directions, 1964), *The Sorrow Dance* (New Directions, 1967), *The Cold Spring and Other Poems* (New Directions, 1968), *Relearning the Alphabet* (New Directions, 1970), *To Stay Alive* (New Directions, 1971), *Footprints* (New Directions, 1972), *The Freeing of the Dust* (New Directions, 1975), and her first book of prose, *The Poet in the World* (New Directions, 1973). Her most recent book of poems is *Life in the Forest* (New Directions, Fall 1978).